D0331190

Keeping
First Things First

John Gile

By the same author:

Minute Meditations

The First Forest

Cover design by Renie Gile

Keeping First Things First

John Gile

First Edition

10   9   8   7   6   5   4   3   2   1

Library of Congress Card Number: 90-084150
ISBN: 0-910941-02-5

Printed in the United States of America
by Worzalla Publishing Co., Stevens Point, Wisconsin

For my teachers,
from an uncooperative student,
with inexpressible gratitude.

J. G.

An Author's Note:

I am a journalist by education and experience, but what I share with you on the following pages comes out of a far more important role I play in life, my role as a husband and a father.

My hope is that you will find something of value in the experiences and reflections I share with you on these pages and, more important, that they will help you realize how much there is of value in you.

I present them to you in random order because they came to me in random order, because life presents itself to us in a somewhat random fashion, and because presenting them without categorization leaves open the possibilty that something here will catch you by surprise.

I am dedicating these pages to some very important people in my life, my teachers. I gave them ulcers. They gave me love. They taught me never, never to give up on anybody, including myself. I can never repay them. All I can do is strive to honor them by passing along to others the help and encouragement they gave me.

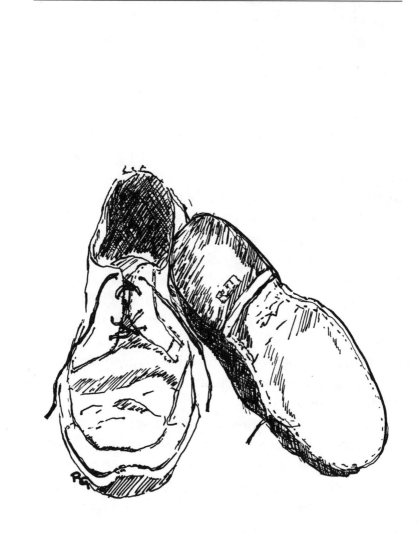

It seems as though
    there is never enough time
        to do all the things
            we have to do.
Or is there?
When I got to work today,
    I realized
        that my shoes weren't shined.
I bent over to shine them at home this morning,
    but heard my little son crying
        before I got the lid off the polish.
So I went to him
    and picked him up
        and dried his tears
            and gave him love.
Then I didn't have time
    to go back and shine my shoes.
I had to leave.
That's okay.
Some day my shoes will be in a scrap heap
    and no one will care
        whether they were ever shined.
But the love I gave my son this morning
    will live on in him
        and those he passes it on to.
No, I'm not embarrassed
    that my shoes aren't shined.
They're a sign that I'm learning
    to keep first things first.

The illusion
    that there will be some time in the future
        when all things will come together for us
           interferes with our fully living today.
If we aren't living fully now,
    we never will.
The only time we ever have
    is the present.

I was a little apprehensive before a recent camping trip because I had read that the bear population was up and the bears were destroying campsites while searching for food. Friends assured me the problems were far north of where we were camping, so I put it out of my mind.

One afternoon, I wandered away from the camp alone to admire the beautiful fall colors. About three miles from camp, what I thought were bear tracks across the trail sent a chill through me. I headed back to camp, fighting an imagination that pictured a bear in every bush.

Then I saw a beautiful sight: one of the camping party was driving down the trail toward me. They had become concerned that I was gone so long. I can't describe the relief I felt.

The experience reminded me how much power we have to help each other — if we just reach out. You never know when a friend may have seen bear tracks across his or her trail.

My four-year-old daughter has a magic body. I told her so. And it's true.

A few days ago she fell off a swing in a friend's yard and cut her hand. It didn't require major medical attention, just a quick washing, a small bandage, routine tear drying, and a few reassuring hugs.

But today we noticed something remarkable: the cut was gone, vanished without a trace. Somehow — like magic — her body had repaired the injured hand, making it like new again.

I know some cynics will come along and tell us it's not magic. They'll tell us that there's a Latin term for it and proceed to give us a boring description of the process.

But that doesn't take away the magic. It just explains how God makes "magic" things happen.

Our trouble is that sometimes we're too dull to recognize God's magic. Imagine if someone made a car that repaired its own dented fenders and scratched paint. The whole world would be excited about it. It would be featured on the news and make headlines around the world.

But God gives us a magic body and we just take it for granted — as we do with so many of our gifts. Lord, please forgive us for being so dull.

You want to change the world?
I can understand that.
I want to change the world, too.
But I believe I can change the world
    not by changing others,
        but by changing myself.

I am writing these notes in the kitchen as I listen to my children bickering and quarreling while they clean up the dishes from our evening meal. Lord, give me patience; give me understanding.

The post-meal carrying on can make me angry, discouraged, depressed, or, on some occasions, all three. It's especially difficult when the older children are in the "negative attitude" stage — hypercritical of their family and impatient with everyone who crosses their paths.

Sometimes they seem to have two personalities: a surly one for the family and a charming one for the telephone. I suspect that is normal. I remember being that way, too. Perhaps the best thing I can do to help them grow out of it is to not be unduly critical of them.

The kitchen is quiet now. All the work is done. The bickering has ended. Harmony is restored. The mood in the home is good. I can stop biting my lip. I am glad You helped me say nothing, Lord. Sometimes that is the best thing to say.

The ability
    to solve problems
       and cope
is nothing more than
    the ability
       to divide and conquer.
The ability
    not to be overwhelmed by a task
is nothing more than
    the ability
       to break it down
          into its smallest parts
           and handle them
              one
              at
              a
              time
                till it's done.

Why is it that,
    when a disagreement arises,
the more wrong I am,
    the louder I yell that I'm right?

We face a constant battle to keep first things first in our lives. Some time ago I didn't have time for anything but work. Then I received an emergency telephone call from my wife: our 18-month-old daughter Elaina had found a container of turpentine and apparently drank some.

Suddenly my work was forgotten. It just didn't matter. Only one thing was important: rushing our daughter to the emergency room. While the doctor examined her, it occurred to me how foolish I am. I was working so hard to earn a living I was losing sight of the very reason for living. The work had become an end in itself. Everything and everyone had become secondary.

The news from the doctor was good. Elaina was fine. Apparently the taste of the turpentine was enough to prevent her from swallowing any. But those anxious moments made me realize that my life, my work, my family — everything and everybody — are God's gifts to me and that one way I show my gratitude is by taking the time to appreciate each of them as they are.

All of us are handicapped in some way.
It may not be something everyone can see,
    but it's there
        in some way
           in all of us.
The only difference is that
    some of us realize it
        and some of us don't.

Knowledge is not the same thing as wisdom.

We can take a frog into a laboratory and dissect it and come away knowing how it croaks and what makes it jump, but in the end we don't have a frog any more — just the parts of a frog.

Humility saves us from the vain idea that our act of acquiring knowledge about God's universe somehow makes us little gods. And humility helps us understand that — as with the frog and all of God's creatures — the whole is sometimes greater than the sum of its parts.

Three considerations foster humility in the truly wise: first, awareness that what we do know is always dwarfed by what we do not know; second, awareness that the very intelligence we use to examine God's universe is a gift from that same God; third, awareness that any of us can dissect a frog, but none of us can create one.

Recently I stood in the kitchen and watched as my small son struggled to push a heavy stool across the floor and up to the counter by the cookie jar. He could have asked me for a cookie. He could have asked me to move the stool for him. But no, he was intent on doing it his way — the hard way.

I thought about how much the relationship of a small child with a parent resembles our relationship with God. How many times have I struggled with problems when help was there for the asking? How many times have I been intent on doing things my way — the hard way?

You and I are like puzzles
    with a missing piece.
And without it
    we can have no peace.
The missing piece
    cannot be filled
        by anything we can buy.
And it cannot be filled
    by our families and friends.
The missing piece in our lives
    is God, our Creator.
And only when we find the missing piece
    can we find peace.

I was listening to a couple old friends solving all the world's problems over lunch recently. I felt sorry for them. Neither has the gift of faith. As I listened, I realized that they live in terribly small, self-centered worlds.

It is as though there's a chair in each of us reserved for God alone. If we shut God out of our lives, that chair is not left empty. It is filled by a little god, usually the god of self. I was both amused and saddened as I saw my friends sitting in God's chair babbling about how they would fix the world. It reminded me of children wearing adult clothing and playing grown-up.

Playing God is a big job and brings with it a lot of burdens and responsibilities we were never meant to bear. It's a lot more fun — and realistic — to live as grateful guests in an incredible world where our challenge is to discern God's will, not dictate it.

I hear talk about how hard it is
    to "give up" this or that —
        and it's true.
But when I curb a vice,
    I'm not giving up anything.
I'm exchanging something "good"
    (at least it seemed good)
        for something better.
And that's much easier.

Lord,
    please give us the wisdom
    to laugh at ourselves.
For only when we can see the humor in life
    can we see the Truth.

For plants and animals,
    one day follows another
        with each day being very much the same
            as the one that preceded it
        and with their habits and habitats
            remaining unchanged through time.
There is repetition in our lives, too:
    the regular pattern of the sun rising and setting,
    the cycles of the seasons,
    and our routine schedules.
But even though the circumstances and events
    may be similar,
        we are changing,
            for better or for worse,
                each day.
We are constantly becoming . . .
    Tomorrow
        we will be
            what we make ourselves
                by what we do today.
We are constantly becoming . . .
    Time lets us grow
        or makes us decay;
            though change we must,
                we choose the way.
We are constantly becoming . . .
    Some persons grow old.
    Others simply grow.

If you'll just let the false gods go,
    the true God will come to you.
If you'll just throw out the trinkets,
    you'll receive the true gold.
There is room in our lives for just one God.

When I pray for a hole in the ground,
the Lord usually answers
by giving me a shovel
and a strong back.

A drop of oil can prolong the lives of machines and motors. The lack of it can bring them to a grinding halt —literally. How often our failure to take less than five minutes to properly oil or maintain machines and appliances results in troubles far out of proportion to the few minutes a little preventive maintenance would have taken.

Prayer is the oil of our lives. It takes only a few seconds to stop and call to mind our Creator, our Source of Life, our Reason for Living. Those few seconds can change so much our attitude toward the day, toward those around us, and toward the difficulties we face.

It is a simple process and it is called keeping first things first.

You don't have to worry.
You only have to do
    the little bit assigned to you
        and the Lord will take care of the rest.
You don't have too much to do:
    you only have too much
        you think you can and must do —
           and that is a form of pride.
Accept your limitations
    and limit your commitments.

There is no such thing as good or bad.
    Good and bad
    are defined
        in relation to the goal or purpose of life.
If there is no goal or purpose,
    then there is no good or bad.
If we have no destination,
    one road is as good to travel as any other.

Even our bodies proclaim the abundant generosity of our Creator.

Medical science tells us two-thirds of both our kidneys could be removed without serious detriment. Normal breathing can be carried on with a large part of our lungs removed.

The thyroid gland has several times the amount of tissue needed for maintaining health. Our adrenal glands produce ten times more adrenalin than we need.

We have about twice as much blood sugar as we normally need for energy. And our hearts and muscles have potential strength far beyond normal needs.

God is so generous in bestowing gifts; why am I so stingy in expressing gratitude?

So often Scripture and religion are used
    as weapons
        to beat people over the head.
They are used
    as threats
        and depictions of the horror that awaits us
            if we do this
                or don't do that.
Instead, they should be presented
    as invitations
        to a full and happy life,
    a promise of joy
        if we accept the invitation.
They are gentle, loving overtures,
    not screaming threats.

Today I ate the most expensive Swedish pancakes with lingonberries I have ever had. On the way to a restaurant my wife and I often visit for a Saturday morning breakfast treat, I made an illegal left turn to escape a traffic jam. A policeman followed us into the parking lot and gave me a ticket with a $50 fine.

I was angry with the policeman and angry with the law and angry because I was caught and — I was just angry. I wasn't very good company for my wife after that, and even the Swedish pancakes didn't taste up to par.

Later it struck me. I did something stupid — and wrong — and then blamed everyone but myself for my trouble.

Lord, save me from fools and save me from folly and save me from fads and fashions. But most of all, Lord, in Your merciful love, save me from my own actions.

We are
    most ridiculous
        when
    we take ourselves
        most seriously.

Babies bring out special qualities in people. Our family at one time extended in age from college to the cradle. One morning after our daughter, Faith, was born, I carried her with me while I went around waking up the older children.

As they opened their eyes, they looked on the face of their new little sister. Each one responded with a smile and a warm greeting. Teenagers don't always wake up that way.

I've seen the same thing happen with coarse, lumberjack types who start smiling and cooing around little ones. It makes me realize things are not always what they seem: some people who have gruff exteriors and sandpaper personalities have hearts as soft as a baby's skin.

It also makes me realize the side of people we see is often a reflection of what they see in us.

I'm blessed with regular helps toward the virtue of humility. The most recent happened the afternoon I took a cup of coffee back to my office after lunch. The only thing I could find to carry it in was one of my children's Walt Disney character thermos bottles.

On my way home from work that evening, I absent-mindedly stopped at a shopping center to drop off some letters at the mailbox there. I got out of the the car and walked to the mail box. As I pulled open the lid to drop in the mail, I realized all I had in my hand was the Disney thermos.

There I stood, looking into the eyes of Mickey Mouse and Pluto and feeling the eyes of every shopper in the area on me.

Thank You, Lord, for never letting me take myself too seriously.

When something makes me really angry
    and I pause to ask myself why,
I often find
    that the things others do
        that most irritate me
    are the very things
        I'm most guilty of myself.

When we frown or scowl,
   we are not at our best.
Frowning and scowling
   are external manifestations
      of an internal disorder.
Somehow we are out of line.
Somehow we are not performing
   as we are designed to perform.
Frowning and scowling are to the mind
   what a fever is to the body:
      a warning.
It's time to stop,
   to change,
      to take care of ourselves,
         to root out the cause.

I narrowly avoided a collision today while I was driving to work. As I entered an intersection with no stop signs, I saw a car approaching from the left. I slammed on my brakes, held on to the steering wheel as my car screeched to a halt, and watched the other car race through *my* right of way.

I was ready to forgive and forget until I saw the driver's face. He was glaring at me — as if I were the one who had done something wrong.

Well, I can overlook having my life placed in jeopardy. And I can overlook someone taking my right of way. But being accused of being in the wrong by someone who clearly is wrong, well — I did a slow burn.

After all, I had saved the ingrate from an accident, from possible injury, from a traffic ticket and a fine, from a hefty repair bill and increased insurance rates, from . . .

My irritation was increased by the sound of a horn blowing. I glanced over my shoulder and realized I was drifting into the lane of a car approaching me from behind.

I also realized that the expression on my face must have been very much like the one on the face of the man at the intersection. Was he really glaring at me? Or was he doing what I just did? Did something happen to irritate him just before he came to the intersection?

Why is it so hard for me to remember, when others irritate me, that I'm not the only person in the world with extenuating circumstances?

On a winter day when snow and ice were thick on city streets, I observed through my window two motorists attempting to get their cars away from the curb and onto the clear center section of the street. The parking area near the curb was covered with thick ice and sloped downward, so the cars had to move uphill a little to reach the area cleared by snowplows.

The first motorist gunned his engine and spun his wheels and went nowhere. The second didn't step on the gas, but let the car slowly edge its way off the ice onto the clear section.

The scene reminded me that, as with the drivers, we need to take our foot off the gas from time to time, no matter how important our work may seem. "Easy does it" sometimes gets the job done, while pressing too hard can leave us spinning our wheels.

What can I give to You, Lord?
The very energy I use,
   the very thought processes I use
   to ask that question
      are a gift from You.
Should I give You all that I am
   I would merely be returning
   what You gave me.

Don't you feel sorry for those who worry about what others think? They're like the couple who drive around town with their car windows up on hot summer days because they don't want the neighbors to know they don't have air conditioning. Can you imagine people inflicting suffering on themselves just to impress others? I can, because sometimes I'm one of them.

I may not go to the extreme described above, but I have the same affliction. Sometimes it shows up as not speaking up when I should. Sometimes it shows up as going along with the crowd when I shouldn't. I always regret it. At best it shows I have more respect for others that I do for myself. At worst it shows I have more regard for people than for God.

The Psalmist tells us we are happy and blessed when we have reverence for God and "walk in God's ways." That doesn't mean we'll be popular.

The more words,
   the less substance:
those who talk much
   say little.

My wife and I nearly drowned in tears the fall we sent our first child, our oldest daughter, off to college. Nobody warned us what a kick in the stomach that can be.

What do you say to someone you first met when she was small enough to hold in one hand? How do you say goodbye to someone you've known and nurtured and cherished for 18 years?

What great words of wisdom do you utter to see her through the days of laughter and days of tears you know lie ahead?

All I could come up with was, "Annie, be yourself." That, and tears — liquid love.

Lord, I've asked for strength to do my part to help our children grow. But now I'm back to ask again — for strength to let them go.

Our philosophies of life
    often evolve from our way of life
        and not vice-versa.
In other words,
    our philosophies of life
        are often mere rationalizations
            for our behavior.
Rather than examining our beliefs
    and thinking about what we should be doing,
we do what we feel like doing
    and then put our minds to work,
        like defense attorneys
            to come up with a good case for us.

The quality of our lives is measured
not by what we have achieved or accumulated,
nor by memories of ourselves we leave behind,
but by the image of You, Lord,
that our relationships with others
leaves with them.

What are you going to do? What are you going to be?

Those are unfair questions we ask our young people. They condemn the young to being preoccupied with life as an end rather than as a process and imply that the young have more control over their lives than is possible for any of us.

The real questions we mean to ask are, "What are you going to be doing?" and "What are you going to spend your time becoming — if you don't change your mind or if events don't compel you to change direction or if your expanded vision from greater experience doesn't cause you to reassess your goals?"

The first questions tend to restrict and put pressure on the young. Oh, yes, by all means, have ambitions, lofty ones. But be aware that living the full, happy life (as far as the human condition permits) involves a great deal of coping, accepting, adapting, and generally growing to love the unpredictable and unforeseen, not because they are lovable, but because they come from One Who loves us.

Resentments can be like clouds hanging over us, blocking out the sun and making life seem gloomy. A friend in Alcoholics Anonymous has a beautiful way of dealing with resentments and converting them into a positive force.

Whenever he gets into a situation that involves negative feelings toward someone, he embarks on a program of prayer for that person. He asks God to bless that person with everything he would like to have in his own life. He said it makes resentment melt away as strong sympathy for the would-be culprit replaces anger.

It reminds me of the story about Abraham Lincoln, who was criticized for his kindness to political opponents. His advisors urged him to destroy his enemies. But Lincoln's response was, "Don't I destroy my enemies when I make them my friends?"

It's when you're on vacation
    or in some other situation
        where you don't have to do anything
    that you find out what you're made of,
        what kind of person you are.
Look at what you do
    when you don't have anything to do
        and you'll catch a glimpse of your soul.

You've been unhappy.
And you've been looking for happiness
    in every corner.
And now you're thinking of doing this or that
    because you think it will make you happy.
And you're right.
    It will make you feel happy —
        for a while.
But when the novelty wears off,
    you'll be right back where you started —
        only worse.
It's like the alcoholic
    who thinks one more drink
        will be the one
            that makes the difference —
                but it never is.
It's not what we do
    that makes us happy or unhappy;
        it's why we do what we do.
It always seems that
    those who seek happiness most
        find it least.
The secret of true happiness is hidden
    within concepts as old as Scripture
        and as modern as the latest psychology text:
            to find your life, you must lose it.
                Simply,
                sincerely,
                selflessly
                    seek to serve others.
Do it as an experiment.
You probably will not find things like
    gratitude, understanding, or reciprocation.
You may not even find the happiness you seek.
But it may find you.

Faith is a gift
    we cannot keep
        unless we share.
And we cannot share it
    without receiving more.

All this excitement,
    all this running,
and all I need is one thing:
    You, Lord.
So why do I bother
    with all the rest?

I recently visited my daughter's eighth grade class to talk with the students about writing and graphic arts. Afterwards, I peeked into the classrooms of my third-grader and kindergartner.

Just seeing them gave me a warm feeling I can only describe as a smile in my heart. Why? Because I love them.

When they noticed me peeking into their rooms, their eyes opened wide and big smiles lit up their faces. The smile in my heart nearly burst as we waved to each other.

When we're feeling discouraged or alone, it might help us to remember that God's eyes are upon us for the same reason my eyes were upon my children in the classrooms, because of a deep and lasting love.

If this world can be so beautiful,
 how much more beautiful
  must its Creator be.
If humankind can be so intelligent
 and accomplish such feats of scientific wonder,
  how much more intelligent
   must humankind's Creator be.
God,
 Source of all beauty,
 Source of all intelligence,
please grant us the gifts
 of understanding,
 appreciation,
 and reverence
  for the beauty of Your world,
   a reflection of Your beauty,
  and for the intelligence
   Your world and creatures manifest,
    reflections of Your intelligence.

Peace is the presence of God.
Where God is not,
   peace is not.

What is evil
        is not necessarily bad.
What is bad
        is not necessarily evil.
It's important to distinguish
        between the two.
Our Lord saves us from evil,
        not from the bad things that happen
                in the normal course of events.
It is bad
        to catch a cold —
                it is not evil.
It is evil
        to be proud and arrogant —
                it is not bad (in today's world).
The definition of bad changes
        from age to age.
Evil is always the same.

Love is a flower
     that blooms
          only in the soil
               of sacrifice.
Where there is no sacrifice,
     there is no love.

We spend much of our time and effort
    striving to be in charge,
    to be on top of things,
        to have everything
        and everybody in our lives
            under control.
But in fact, we control little in our lives.
None of us has made a decision to be born.
None of us has decided
    where to be born
    or when
    or of whom.
None of us has selected
    the talents we have
    and the talents we don't have
    or the difficulties and opportunities
        we meet in our lifetimes.
Nor do any of us control, ultimately,
    our health
    or our relative longevity.
In the natural course of human life,
    we are simply at the mercy of elements
    beyond our control.
Lord, You give us lives
    filled with days of laughter
        and days of tears.
Please give us
    the humilty to accept our limitations,
    the strength to endure tribulation,
    and the wisdom to make the best of our lives
        by helping others make the best of theirs.

The young are always campaigning
    for a new social order
        that promises
            peace,
            happiness,
            and prosperity
                for everyone.
And there's nothing wrong with that.
Our young should see visions.
But "they all lived happily ever after"
    is fairy tale material,
        not realistic, social planning.
The problem isn't so much
    that the system is failing the people
        as it is that the people are failing the system.
Don't place too much hope
    in the creation of a new social order,
        because, even if one is established,
            it'll be made up of people
                with the same old human nature.

It is unfortunate
    that we equate education
    with degrees.
That is like
    equating justice
    with law
        or wisdom
        with knowledge
            or faith
            with religion.
Very often, in fact,
    they have little to do with each other.

The world sets me in a struggle
  against my true nature
    as it fosters the illusion
      that I am self-sufficient.
And as I struggle
  against my true nature,
    I experience
      conflict,
      anxiety,
      and fear.
In quiet moments before our Lord,
  I am freed
    from that illusion.
In quiet moments before our Lord,
  the sand of self-confidence
    is replaced
  by the rock of God-confidence.
In quiet moments before our Lord,
  conflict and anxiety and fear
    give way to peace
      beyond expression.
The world inflicts wounds upon us
  which God alone can heal.
In quiet moments before our Lord,
  I experience
    that healing power
    and catch a glimpse
      of the divine compassion
        we are called to share.
In the presence of the Source of life,
  I am made aware
    that all of life
      is a gift
        to be humbly accepted
        and appreciated.
Thank You, Lord,
  for quiet moments of prayer.

My father was scheduled for open heart surgery within a week. He was in a weakened condition and had been sent home from the hospital for a time to build up his strength for the surgery.

One of my uncles, a kind and prayerful man, was worried about him. He stopped in often to visit with my father and see how he was coming along.

One afternoon, after visiting for an hour or so, my uncle went home and sat in his favorite chair to watch a baseball game on television. Moments later he slumped over in the chair and died, suddenly and completely without warning. All the while that my uncle was worrying about my father dying, his own death had been rapidly approaching.

The story is not unusual. Almost everyone knows of friends and relatives who have had a physical checkup and are pronounced in perfect health only to die suddenly within minutes of leaving the doctor's office. Daily news reports are filled with stories of untimely deaths from accidents, floods, earthquakes, and so on — all telling us that we have only the present moment and no more that we can count on, all reminding us to treasure each moment of each day and every person who comes our way.

Happiness and fulfillment
   are by-products
      of doing our work
      and meeting
         our duties,
         obligations,
         commitments,
         and responsibilities.
For it is in meeting them
   that we meet God.

Don't do anything
  if you can't do it with love.
Silence is better
  than a hateful remark.

"Power to the people!"
That sounds good,
    but watch out.
What the people who shout it often mean
    is "Power to me"
        or "Power to my group"
            or "Power to my particular cause"
at the expense of everybody else.

What we call the ordinary, everyday world
    is full of some pretty startling surprises.
Who would ever expect
    to see things like
        red tomatoes,
        yellow corn,
        green peppers,
        and purple grapes
            coming from the same brown earth?
And how about the idea
    of getting
        white milk
        from
        black cows
            that eat green grass?
Sometimes reality
    is more like a fairy tale
        than most fairy tales.
The only surprising thing
    is that we are so slow
        to recognize and trust
            the One behind it all.

Belief in God
    is not just an agreement
        with certain philosophical arguments
        and theological propositions.
It is a personal relationship
    with the Person of God.
It would be more correct
    to say, "I know God"
        than to say, "I believe in God."

When will we learn,
    in our efforts at social engineering,
        that there are no social solutions
            to spiritual problems?

Many persons I know
    have much higher callings
        than they realize
    but live on much lower levels
        than they should.
Our perceptions
    determine our attitudes.
And our attitudes
    increase
    or
    diminish
        the joy we experience
        and give to others.
Men and women in every walk of life
    seek fulfillment.
But fulfillment isn't something
    we get from our work.
It is something
    we bring to it.
Fulfillment isn't found
    in what we do,
        but in why we do it.

Get rid of your
	bitterness
	jealousy,
	anger,
	and hate,
not only for what
	they do to others,
but for what
	they do to you.

I was awakened early one summer morning by a strange sensation in my chest. My heart seemed to be fluttering, then pounding vigorously, then fluttering again.

I walked around the room, hoping the feeling would pass. It didn't. I asked my wife to listen to my chest and see if it sounded as strange as it felt. It did. I grew weaker. We decided to go to the hospital.

At the emergency room, a nurse listened to my heartbeat and confirmed something was wrong. Within minutes I found myself on a hospital bed with wires attached to my chest and arms and legs. Doctors and nurses came and went, asking questions and taking blood samples.

I remember feeling disbelief. What am I doing here? This is something that happens to other people. I was angry, not at anyone, but at my situation. I was sad, near tears, thinking of my wife and children. Am I dying? Am I leaving them? And I was worried about my work, my deadlines.

But the most overwhelming feeling of all was one of utter powerlessness. There was nothing I could do but lie there and pray.

The diagnosis was good: no heart attack, just an extremely erratic heartbeat brought on by too much coffee, too much stress, too little rest and exercise. I was home within hours, determined to change my habits, more thankful than ever for the gift of life, and more aware than ever of my ultimate powerlessness and dependence.

We are called to praise God,
　　to give thanks to God.
That theme is repeated
　　again and again
　　　　throughout Scripture.
This is not the command
　　of an egomaniac who craves or needs praise.
This is something for our good.
We are somehow at our best
　　when we are thanking God.
When we are thanking God,
　　we are swimming with the current,
　　we are in tune with reality.
It is when we fail
　　to give thanks to God in all things
　　　　that we are going against the current
　　　　and are out of step with reality.
It is then that we make the mistake
　　of trying to step in
　　　　and play God.
But we just aren't big enough
　　to play that role.
"Praise the name of the Lord," the Psalmist says,
　　not only because it is right and just,
　　　　but because it is for our own good.

All of life is by nature fleeting:
    a beautiful sunrise,
    autumn leaves,
    a tender touch.
We cannot capture them forever.
It is folly to try.
We can only appreciate them.

If we had more,
 I fear we would have less;
  for even now it is impossible
   to truly appreciate all we have.
Our appetites are limitless
 and satisfying them intensifies cravings.
What we want impatiently today
 we treat indifferently tomorrow.
What we think we cannot live without today
 we gladly throw away tomorrow.
Having too much
 may turn out to be
  the most abject poverty of all.

Being honest to God,
  being sincere in prayer,
    sometimes means praying in anger.
If we are going to bring God everything,
  all our hopes
  fears,
  needs,
  joys —
  everything —
    it follows that
      we must bring our anger, too.
After all, didn't the same God
  Who created our capacity
      for joy
      and hope
      and love
  also create our capacity
      for anger?
And can sane persons,
  beholding the state of the world,
  beholding the way we mistreat each other,
    not grow angry,
      even, at times, angry with God?
Acknowledging our anger
  is being honest with ourselves.
Expressing our anger,
  constructively, without personal attacks,
    is being honest with others.
And praying in anger
  is just being honest to God.

The suffering in our lives
is the labor pain we must endure
in giving birth to wisdom.

Look out for self-pity.
It is one of the most
   overlooked,
   powerful,
   devastating,
   clever,
   insidious
      forms of evil —
         because it is not recognized as evil.
It gets past our guard,
   distorts reality,
   and provokes anger.
Self-pity takes away our sense of humor,
   shuts down communication,
     and stifles our creative powers.
It makes us concentrate on ourselves,
   miss the good we could be doing for others,
     and blocks out the voice of God.
Letting all that happen to us
   is what makes self-pity so pitiful.

When I am aware of the presence of God, I have music in my soul. How can I describe it?

Imagine yourself in the middle of a large city during rush hour in one of the city's worst traffic jams on the hottest day of the year. Stalled cars are clogging traffic flow. Cars are changing from one lane to another and back again, brakes are screeching, drivers are being rude to each other, horns are blowing, tempers flaring.

Picture yourself, however, driving along in no particular rush and listening to a tape of your favorite music. Your car is comfortable and air conditioned. You are involved in the confusion and chaos — but also are apart from it.

That is what the peace of the presence of God is like — order within disorder, alert relaxation, energetic calm — peace, even amidst strife.

It seems strange to me
    that we must spend so much time and effort
        trying to teach unwilling children to read.
If they could be made to understand
    what worlds open to them with that skill,
        they would teach themselves.
I wonder if God looks on us
    in our foolishness
        the same way.

Are we praying for peace?
Or are we praying for an end to fighting?
Peace does not mean
    performing a frontal lobotomy
        on the human race.
That's not peace — that's silence.
True peace can be noisy and confusing.
That's because true peace
    is not the absence of turmoil and disagreements.
Peace is the absence
    of injustice and bitterness and hate.
Prayers for peace
    may be answered
        in a strong resolve
            to oppose evil.
And that can involve us
    in struggle
    and persecution.
The world can take away our comfort.
But it is powerless to make us stop loving,
    to drive out the presence of God,
        to destroy the peace only God can give.
The greatest threat to peace
    may not be the arms in the world;
    but the absence of God in our hearts.

Improvement should be your goal,
    not perfection.
Life is a process;
    improvement is a process.
Constant improvement
    is the perfection
        of the process of living.

Challenges make us grow.
It is only when we are doing something difficult
    that we are growing.
It is only by lifting heavy weights
    that we develop our muscles.
Life's challenges are our opportunities for growth
    and reminders of God's love for us.

"Rejoice."
"Have a light heart."
Those are the Psalmist's commands.
Fear?
Anxiety about the future?
Those are sure ways
    to stunt our spiritual growth.
We have the present moment,
    and that's all.
Do what you must do now
    and then rest your mind.

If we really understood,
if we really realized
    all that our Lord
        has in store for us
    and all that our Lord
        is constantly doing for us,
then, even in what seems to be our darkest hour,
    our only prayer would be,
        "Thank You."

Happiness is a by-product
    of being exactly what God created us to be.
And what's that?
    Intelligent.
    Kind.
    Free.
    Helpful.
    Prayerful.
    Sincere.
    Grateful.
    Open.
    Honest.
    Loving.
In short,
    fully human,
    fully alive.

Gratitude.
Two receive a gift.
Both say thanks.
Later the two are observed.
One has cared for the gift
and it still looks like new.
The other has neglected the gift
and abused it till it is barely recognizable.
Which one was truly grateful?
All we are and have — even life itself —
is a gift from our Creator.
To be thankful for our gifts
requires more than words.
Are we grateful for our bodies?
Our homes?
Our jobs?
Our lives?
What do our actions show?
Words are cheap.
Our actions show
what's in our hearts.

Just imagine what the world would be like
        if we really worked
                to see that others
                        are better off than we are.
Just imagine.
What would we have to fight about?
        About who could be the most generous?
        About who could be the least selfish?
Just imagine.
Just imagine what the world would be like
        if we took pleasure
                in what we do for others each day
        rather than in what we have done
                or gained for ourselves.
Just imagine.
        What would cause us anxiety?
        What would happen to resentment?
        What would we worry about?
Just imagine.

Of course it's not easy.
Do you expect to be
    the first person on the face of the earth
    who escapes the scrapes and bruises,
        both physical and emotional,
    that sharing the human condition brings?
Do you think you can selectively partake
    of the joys and pleasures of life
        but forego the trials and tribulations?
Be realistic.
Embrace life — all of it.
    Comfort,
    self-indulgence,
    escape,
    the easy life —
those are illusions,
    exit signs along the road of life
        that lead nowhere.
The more we seek ourselves,
    the smaller our world becomes
    and the larger our troubles become.

Bookstores have large sections
    of what claim to be self-help books
        inviting us to be "no-limit" persons
            who are healthy,
            wealthy,
            wise,
            and perpetually young.
When I see them,
    I think of the serpent in Genesis
        promising, "You shall be as gods."
It seems strange
    that millions of those books have been sold,
        but I have never met or heard of anyone
            who became a "no-limit" person
                by reading them.
Everyone I know
    has limited time,
    limited talents,
    limited means,
    limited health,
    and a limited life span.
That's because the authors of those books
    cannot give to others
        what they don't have themselves.
God alone
    is the Source of all we seek.

Sometimes I'm a forgetful father, forgetting all that has been done for me. I'm forgetful when I look at the family room and yell, "Look at the mess you've made. Clean up this place. Put those toys away right now!"

Then I play the role of whip-cracking slave driver. The result is reluctant cooperation. It gets the job done, but it leaves hard feelings all over the place.

On other occasions, I may say, "Wow, this place is a mess. Let's pick things up." And then I join in the restoration of order. The result is greater cooperation. It can even be fun for both the little ones and me.

I receive so much help and forgiveness for the big messes I make; helping my children clean up their little messes is the least I can do.

Getting down on my knees to pick up toys may be the best prayer I can say.

Lord,
   help us remember
      we can never learn
         to put first things first
            until we learn
               to put ourselves last.

Some day I want to write a book called "Things I'd Like To Tell My Children, But They Probably Wouldn't Listen Anyway."

One of the things I would like to remind my children about in that book is that late in life we come to pay the price for mistakes we make early in life.

Space launches teach the lesson well. A mistake made early in the launch near the earth, a mistake of only inches or even fractions of an inch will, if uncorrected, send the space vehicle off course by thousands of miles in later flight.

Our lives are like that. We are setting a course today by what we do — and by what we fail to do. What is true in the area of work habits, physical conditioning, self-control, is equally true in the realm of faith.

When we are faced with a crisis some distant day and need strong faith to see us through, we will have it then only if today we ask for it, nourish it, and cherish it.

Almost any day we can read the front page of the newspaper and ask, "How can God let this happen?" or "Where is God?" It is as if we expect God to appear on the scene in the form of a caped crusader to fight the forces of evil and set everything straight.

That is great for a TV story or a movie script, but Scripture and experience tell us that is not the way the real world works.

We are the ones who make or fail to make God's presence felt in the world by what we do or fail to do. World events are merely large scale versions of what is happening on the individual level in our relationship with our Lord and with our families and friends and co-workers.

The question is not "Where is God?" The question is "What have we done to make God present?" Let there be peace and justice on earth, Lord, and let it begin with me.

Almost all the happiness we know in life
is born in suffering.
Almost all joy
is born in pain.
The joy of birth
is preceded by the agony of labor and delivery.
The joy of learning
is born of the agony of self-discipline and study.
The joy of victory
is born of the agony of training and competition.
It often seems
that the greater the difficulty,
the greater our joy in overcoming it.
Overprotective parents miss that.
Protecting children from adversity
denies them opportunities to know
feelings of accomplishment and self-worth
that are among life's richest treasures.
Maybe that is why
we are allowed to experience
so many troubles
in our lives.

Lord,
    please cleanse our minds
        of society's opinions
            concerning good and bad.
For what society calls good
    is often simply the easy
and what society calls bad
    is often simply the difficult.
Please help us remember
    that doing the easy
        often creates difficulties
    while doing the difficult
        brings ease.

Afterthoughts . . .

If you're like most people I know,
   you probably don't realize
      how good you are
      and how much you are loved.
And you probably try too hard to do too much,
   as though you were all alone.
If God came into your room today
   and sat down in a chair across from you,
      and began to speak to you,
         I think this is what God would say:
"You seem to think you are in charge,
   but you're not.
You are working for me.
You are doing tasks I assign.
Remember that.
And remember that I stand ready

to help you
　　with whatever your need —
　　　　my strength,
　　　　my wisdom,
　　　　my means.
So don't worry.
Just try to do
　　the things I ask you to do
　　　　directly or through my messengers.
And relax.
I never give you too much to do
　　or assign heavy tasks
　　　　without giving you
　　　　　　all the help you need to do them.
And there is enough time
　　to do the things I assign —
　　　　if you don't try to cram in
　　　　　　your own pet projects.
You are responsible to me alone.
Remember, I'm on your side,
　　I'm with you
　　　　and I'm always ready to help.
You are never alone — never.
Your "to-do" list is from me
　　and should be a source of joy,
　　　　not of anxiety.
If you do feel anxiety,
　　you're forgetting everything I've said.
I'm giving you
　　everything you need
　　　　when you need it —

even though sometimes it doesn't appear so
and you don't understand what I'm doing.
Trust me.
I know what is best for you
and want what is best for you
more than anyone else in the world —
including you yourself.
Trust me.
And come to me frequently.
I'm with you,
walking before you,
directing you.
Even when you pray,
it is my impulse you're receiving,
my call you are answering.
The very fact
that you even think of praying
is a sign that I am with you.
You are my child.
My blood flows through your veins.
I am proud of you
and sympathetic with you.
I will help you constantly
and in all things —
if you just let me.
You focus on the process,
do your best to do your duty
and let me worry about the results.
You plow the field and sow the seed —
I'll make things grow."